MW01227988

THE MILLIONAIRE MAKER

THE MILLIONAIRE MAKER

Six Practical Steps to Your First Four Homes

CHRIS STORY

ISBN: 979-8-9852696-4-2 (soft cover)
ISBN: 979-8-9852696-6-6 (hard cover)
ISBN: 979-8-9852696-5-9 (ebook)

Story Productions LLC
1005 Carriage Court
Homer Alaska 99603
907.299.7653
AlaskaMattersRadio@gmail.com
www.ILoveHomerAlaska.com

Printed in the United States

For Tiffanie, the love of my life,
best friend and business partner!

CONTENTS

STEP 6

More Valuable
Than GOLD

It was a typical Wednesday morning at the pottery shop. Wet clay had taken shape as bowls, plates, and trivets, while other pots were still cooling in the kiln after being glaze-fired to over 2,000 degrees. No customers were present when my dad walked in.

He looked around. Seeing no one, he said, "Come with me; I want to show you something." Incredulous, I responded, "But Dad, the store is open. I can't just leave."

Once again, he surveyed the empty store, smiled, and said, "Come on. We won't be long."

I grabbed my jacket and put up the "Will be back" sign on the door, locked up, and jumped into his still idling Suburban.

"Where are we going?" I asked.

"To the future," Dad said. Okay, he didn't say that, but wouldn't it have been awesome if he had?

The truth is, he said nothing. He drove onto the main road, crossed the highway towards the beach, slowed down, and turned into a short driveway stub of a vacant lot. Then he said, "You and Tiffanie should buy this; then let's build you guys a building of your own."

My heart went into panic mode, practically beating out of my chest. The idea of buying land and then constructing a commercial building was so far outside my comfort zone, I simply couldn't even entertain the thought.

He might as well have suggested I flap my arms and fly to the treetops. I made all kinds of excuses he didn't accept.

Dad didn't argue with me. He simply said, "I'll help you. You can do this."

Now, he didn't mean he'd help me financially. He meant he would help us logistically. Rather than lend us money, he would lend us know-how, and just as importantly, a belief in ourselves. Last but not least, Dad also lent us relationships. By standing with us as we made this first investment, he was telling the realtor, the bank, and the title company that we were a solid risk. His credibility rubbed off on us.

Although not born with a silver spoon, I'm the first to admit that what my dad lent Tiffanie and I was invaluable, and perhaps more valuable than a deep pocket.

Throughout this simple guide to wealth, you'll learn how to set yourself up for a lifetime of riches. You'll be able to borrow my belief in you and leverage the relationships I've spent thirty years building.

Some of the concepts in this guide might sound strange at first. Please set aside your disbelief, act as if you're at a movie, and let the images, ideas, and practices come to life in your mind. Soon enough, you'll be starring in your own feature film. You have what it takes to succeed in real estate. How do I know? You are holding this book. You clearly have a thirst for knowledge. You are destined to attain what you want, control your destiny, and leave a lasting legacy.

This is the exact right time, and you are in the perfect place!

Let's get started.

Decide: Make Up Your Mind to Become a Millionaire

Failure will never overtake me if my determination to succeed is strong enough.

— Og Mandino

Decide
from the Latin *decidere*—literally "to cut off"

To access the millions of acres of Alaskan back-country, you would be wise to own an Argo (an 8-wheeled All-Terrain Track Vehicle). The Argo I had was unstoppable. Try as I might, I couldn't get it stuck. Through bogs and marsh-land, large ponds to steep embankments, the Argo would go and go.

Then one day, a hub broke on one of the eight wheels. This was a mechanical issue be-yond my very limited abilities. A quick call to my friend John Calhoun, and the invitation to come to his well-equipped shop was extended. I knew once John was involved, the issue was already solved.

We worked and worked on freeing up the bolts keeping the wheel in place. They seized and refused to budge. After a solid hour of try-ing, I threw up my hands and said, "Thanks anyway, John. I'll take her in to the shop and have them make the repair."

John put down the wrench he'd been pull-ing against with all his might and looked at me. He said, "Oh, I thought you wanted to do this." He didn't bother to hide his disgust at my willingness to quit so easily. Oh wow, that was a gut check. I said, "Yeah, but this is really hard."

John replied with something that I've never forgotten, "If you're committed, then we can see this through. If not, go ahead and leave." We worked on it for another half hour before the first bolt gave way to our efforts. With one done, the other bolts came loose shortly thereafter. A little like Roger Bannister breaking the impossible four-minute mile, only to have dozens follow in his fast footsteps and likewise do the impossible.

In the words of Les Brown regarding breakfast, "The chicken was involved, but the pig . . . he was committed." (In the above story, I guess that makes my friend John the pig. ☺)

If you commit to the goal of becoming a millionaire, you're halfway there. The other five steps will teach you the path to follow. But the first step of this journey towards wealth and independence starts with the decision. Cutting off from all other options.

As you set foot on this path towards becoming a millionaire, you must commit. To make the commitment more tangible, use visualization. The science is in, there is zero doubt concerning the power of visualization. It works.

Commitment: *Sixty percent of the time, it works every time.*
— Brian Fantana, Anchorman

How to Visualize

Get in a quiet space, preferably alone. Use headphones to cancel room noise if you can't isolate. Also, it's nice to add in a little Zen music with some background of running water. This triggers a sense of tranquility, allowing your mind to open. Once you are situated comfortably, begin with a mantra.

For example: "I'm a millionaire in the making. I'm happily owning and managing four homes that create cash flow and earn money while I sleep."

Repeat your mantra over and over until your mind is clear of any other thoughts. As you recite, visualize a home on a tree-lined sunny street (or a duplex or four-plex). Imagine people coming and going from a front door that's freshly painted. What color is the door? What color is the house? It's your visualization—add details and features that make you happy. Once you have the picture in your mind, imagine someone coming out of the door with a check in hand. See your hand reaching out for the check. You take it, look closely. The check is made out to you in the amount of (fill in the blank with a number of your choosing) dollars. You smile at the person and walk on down the street to the next house. Same as before. A happy and smiling person emerges with another check, also made out to you. Keep walking, keep collecting checks.

Sharon Lechter, co-author of the *Rich Dad Poor Dad* series, has a saying, "Assets are sexy." Yes, they are. These homes you are visualizing are assets. Your assets that will continue to make you money 24/7/365. Imagine each as your own private ATM. Printing you money over and over. We'll talk about the details of the "how" throughout the remainder of this guide. What's foundational, and most important, is your commitment to becoming a millionaire. Use this visualization exercise to affirm your commitment and bolster your belief in yourself. Remember, if I can do this . . . so can you!

Assemble Your Team— Become the CEO of YOU, Inc.

You are the average of the five people you spend the most time with.

— Jim Rohn

In my book, *The Backyard Millionaire*, Oscar (the backyard millionaire) schools young August in the ways of his inner circle. No, not his inner child. Wrong book.

Oscar draws a circle on his placemat and asks August how many circles he sees. Naturally, August says there's only one circle. He soon learns the error of his ways. This was a tough lesson for me to learn over the years. The fact of the matter is that we have two circles in our lives. One of proximity, the circle of colleagues or fellow employees (students), and then the inner circle, the group we allow to hold influence in our lives, consciously, and on purpose.

The elephant in the room is that the outer circle may, in fact, attend the same family reunions as you. Yes, I'm talking about your own family. While you contemplate your circle of influence in your life, be honest. Who is feeding into your life's hopes and dreams? And who is feeding you a banquet of fear, doubt, and dubious advice masquerading as concern? As discussed in *The Backyard Millionaire*, you can't always cut the negative people out of your life. But you certainly don't have to let them inside the inner circle.

So, as you assemble your Millionaire Support Team, look for people who are positive, knowledgeable, and most importantly, have been there and done that (whether they bought the T-shirt or not). Before I give you the exact list of who you'll want on your team, a word of caution: Be careful who you tell your plans to. There are people in your circle of proximity who love nothing more than to dump poison into open ears, that can spill over into your heart and kill off ambition and your fledgling momentum.

Share your millionaire plan only with those you are sure will support you and can offer real-world aid in your cause. When you have enough momentum and road behind you, then you can shout your desires from the top of the world, and no one can get in between you and your goals. But in the beginning, guard your back by forming a tight-knit team. That team should consist of:

+ Trusted real estate broker: (a Realtor®)
+ Qualified local mortgage broker
+ Licensed home inspector (with practical building experience)
+ Contractor: specialty or general

+ Hard money lender: private finance
+ Banker: your local bank
+ Handyman service provider
+ Licensed electrician
+ Licensed plumber
+ Maintenance pros: from painting to flooring installation
+ Real estate attorney
+ Mentor (an investor willing to be your guide)

How to Assemble Your Team

So, you want to build a team?

Notice who's at the top of the list? Yes, your real estate broker. Also, notice that the broker should be a Realtor®. Long and short of that is, realtors are licensed to sell real estate, but have also taken extra measures to adhere to a code of ethics that dates back over 100 years. In addition, realtors are held to higher standards of practice than is required by law. In

some instances, judges have adjudicated cas-
es holding the realtor accountable to our very
own code of ethics. Once you've made the ac-
quaintance of a trusted real estate professional,
you now have your gateway into the rest of
your team. If for any reason you are unsure
of who to work with, ask around. You'll hear
a name or two pop up more than any others;
that's a good place to start.

Or please contact me, and I will help connect you to a qualified realtor in your backyard, who has experience with investors (www.
ILoveHomerAlaska.com).

With your list in hand, ask your real estate broker for recommendations to fill out
your team. You'll undoubtedly get at least two
names for each team member.

NOTE: If they can't supply you with names
and contacts, RUN; you're in the wrong
place. Keep looking for the right real estate
broker. A qualified broker works with all of

these people on a regular basis and will have great relationships with other qualified professionals you'll need to know. This is why you connect with your realtor first!

Remember you are interviewing people who will work for you. So even if you don't have any jobs for them currently, take a few minutes with potential team members, get to know them. Ask for some references and take the time to follow up with those past customers. Past performance most certainly does predict future results.

When you have the need for service from any team member, it's absolutely imperative that you pay them swiftly. You want your team to look forward to your calls. Make your requests for service clear, concise, and payment upon completion, or as close as possible thereafter. When you've assembled the right team, you won't have to bargain or beat them down on price. You'll know you're getting more in use value from them than you are paying in cash value.

Ready — Set — Unite!

My Next Step:

_____

_____

_____

_____

_____

_____

_____

_____

_____

_____

_____

_____

Get Prequalified: Know What You Can Do—Then You Can Do What You Want To Do

Knowledge is power.

— Francis Bacon

One day, Tiffanie and I went to look at a house. We loved this house. The backyard was an ideal place for a child to play. Surrounded by a tall wooden fence, it was private and secure. A variety of mature trees dotted the property. On that summer day, we could already envision the piles of golden and red leaves that would gently float to the lawn. The blanket of fresh snow that would follow washed over our imagination, with roly-poly snowmen, and so many other visions of watching our daughters' play, carefree. The thing about the imaginative playground we created is that's exactly where it stayed—our imagination. You see, the house we fell in love with was beyond our financial means.

You naturally ask, why were you even there? How did you not know it was out of reach? Exactly. We had been led by a well-intentioned, nevertheless clueless agent. She allowed us to fall in love with what wasn't an option, thus coloring every other property we were able to qualify for with a layer of resentment at not being the one we actually wanted.

STOP

You're not going to be painting images in the sky of your mind about these homes like we naively did. However, you still need to know, as an investor, what you can do, so you can determine what you want to do as it pertains to return on investment (ROI). You will learn a lot about the mortgage world simply by going through the process of getting prequalified. It'll cost you nothing. Yes, you read that correctly. Zero. A little time invested here to really understand the process, and what loan type you're qualifying for will pay you back a hundredfold. This is why selecting the right mortgage lender is so vital.

Ask your real estate broker for a few names they like to work with. Both with your real estate broker and mortgage broker, you're looking for someone who is willing to invest time in you and help with your education. This, after all, is going to be a long-term relationship. I've worked exclusively with one mortgage broker for the past twenty-two years. Rhonda Johnson is like a business partner to Team Story (truth be told, she has become like an extension of our family)

Remember also there are as many creative ways to finance as you can imagine. Working with your Realtor, you can explore owner financing as well as some private hard money lenders. Whenever possible you'll want to avoid balloon payments, or what many call "debt bombs."

As an investor, you want the property to pay itself off over time, versus you having to come up with a large amount of cash at some point to satisfy the "call due" or balloon payment.

Get prequalified—then get ready to launch into your best life!

MY NEXT STEP

_____

_____

_____

_____

_____

_____

_____

_____

_____

_____

_____

_____

_____

_____

_____

_____

_____

_____

_____

_____

_____

_____

_____

_____

_____

STEP 4

Learn the Market— In Your Own Backyard.

Never become so much of an expert that you stop gaining expertise.

View life as a continuous learning experience.

— Denis Waitley

"Do you know what this would sell for if it was in California?" (or pick a state where the property in question isn't). The reality is, right there in your own backyard, multiple markets exist. This is something that I remind new buyers in our area of all the time.

There are as many markets as there are property types and unique areas. For our purposes of moving you into backyard-millionaire status, let's focus on the "residential-rental" real estate market in your backyard. This means we are going to focus on those homes that best lend themselves to the rental pool in your area. This will vary from town to town and state to state.

Allow me to help you jump ahead in the line of life through a mistake we made in this department. The best kind of mistakes are other people's, right? (So long as you learn from them.)

One day a very kind older woman came to see me. She was in a pinch and needed to sell in a hurry. For a variety of reasons, including health, she wanted to vacate the area quickly and without a lot of fuss. This presented an opportunity for Tiffanie and me to step in as investors and help her out, and in the process pick up a fine rental property. The house needed a significant face-lift, one that she couldn't afford, nor did she have the time to wait for upgrades even if she'd had the cash. We negotiated a deal that was fair to all concerned (a topic we will discuss in Step 5). Once we closed, we rolled up our sleeves and went to work. Between the two of us, a budget of $15,000, and a lot of hard work later, we banged out a very nice rental. We stepped back and took stock of what we'd done. By God, it was perfect! A real transformation worthy of a feature on an episode of PBS's *This old house*. It wasn't until we looked up from the work we had done that we noticed the fatal flaw in our plan. We had ignored the market. We hadn't given credence to the fact that this was the best home in the area. An area that was virtually surrounded by multifamily apartments that rented at a fraction of what we would need to charge for our newly renovated single-family home. We had a sinking feeling we'd made an error.

Months of vacancy later (while waiting for the tenant willing to pay the price we needed), we realized we were always going to struggle with this property. So, we cut our losses and resold the home in its shiny condition. It took months to sell, and when it finally sold, it was for less than if it had been located in an area with similar homes. We were able to recoup our money, at least most of it (if you don't count the carried mortgage costs during the period of renovation and vacancy). This is where my revisionist history battles it out with Tiffanie's command of the actual budget and bottom line. She still swears we lost money on that one. What we agree on is this: *We will never buy the nicest (rental) house in a neighborhood again.*

How to Learn The Market In Your Backyard

First of all, recognize the differing markets you've got in your area. The markets will be segregated out by amenities, proximity from city center, and price/size/scale. Your first step to learn your market locally: Ask your realtor to set you up on a drip feed from the Multiple Listing Service (MLS).

You will be fed any/all new listings or price changes via email immediately. Begin also to pay attention to what is coming on the market in an area you've selected for investment. How long do homes stay on the market? Can you discern what the list-to-sell ratio is (ask your realtor for data)?

Notice the neighboring properties—are they predominantly rentals or owner-occupied? My preference is to locate my rentals in owner-dominated neighborhoods. You'll benefit from the pride of ownership and stability that these areas provide. While you are studying the real estate sales market, get a handle on the rental market too. What's vacant? What do 3-bedroom 2-bath homes rent for versus 2/1, or 1/1? We have learned from experience that

1/1 can be more prone to vacancy, whereas the 3/1.5 to 3/2 rent out faster, tenants stay longer, and pay higher rent. At some point, you will have your four homes, you will be managing them and have your millionaire plan in place. Then you may wish to dip your toe into multifamily properties. So, while you are studying the single-family market, pay attention to what's going on in the multifamily market too. We now enjoy investing in and owning apartment buildings, duplexes, commercial buildings, mini-storage, and single-family homes. We are experts in our local market; ironically though, I can't tell you anything about the market sixty miles to the north of me.

We are after all: "backyard" millionaires.

My Next Step

_____

_____

_____

_____

_____

_____

_____

_____

_____

_____

_____

_____

_____

Master Negotiations— The Art Of Getting What You Want

Master negotiations by caring . . . but not thaaaaaat much.

— Herb Cohen

When I was a kid, my dad would travel outside for meetings and sales conferences. (Among Alaskans, contiguous America is referred to as Outside—also The Lower 48.) I remember him coming home one year and talking about the great negotiator Herb Cohen. No idea why that stuck out in my mind. But many years later, after I had become a real estate broker, I came across Herb's fantastic book: *You Can Negotiate Anything*, which led me to his masterwork, *Negotiate This*.

Having read Cohen's books and employed his techniques for many years, I decided to reach out to him. On a whim, I searched him out on the internet, found his website, and shot off an email to the "contact us" button.

Within an hour of sending that email, my phone rang. To my shock, the caller ID announced a number from New York, New York. Wow! The Big Apple was calling! Could it be? No. It was surely not Herb Cohen, negotiator to US presidents, the man the FBI consulted for hostage negotiations, and lead negotiator for global corporations.

"Hello?"

"Chris, it's Herb Cohen calling."

Oh my God! It was Herb.

"Herb, I can't believe you're calling me. I just emailed you not that long ago."

"Chris, your email was compelling. How could I not call?"

We had a fantastic conversation about life and negotiations. I invited him to be my guest on my *On Top of the World* radio show. He graciously accepted, and we set a date.

Herb granted me a full hour of his time for that interview. We talked about his best friend from childhood, Larry King, and he shared fabulous stories about his many years of negotiations.

What I'm about to share with you now is only the tip of the iceberg. My goal is whetting your appetite for mastering the art of negotiations. From here, I recommend grabbing a copy of *Negotiate This* by Herb Cohen. While you're at it, grab his other book *Everything's Negotiable*. Chester Karrass wrote extensively on the subject of negotiation as well. He coined the phrase, "You don't get what you want in life, you get what you negotiate." Study, learn, and most importantly, practice negotiating.

Begin to use the art of negotiation in your life right *now*. While the bar is relatively low, start practicing.

Negotiation 101

TIP: Time — Information — Price

Time. Notice that time comes before price. This means both the timing in the market and the timing in your life. When the prices fell through the floor in the Las Vegas real estate market, it was the wrong time in my life to take advantage. Timing the market with your timing in life is critical. Also, controlling the time in a deal. Make sure you're not rushed into any hasty decisions. There will always be another deal. If you feel that time is being used against you by the other side or some other player in the transaction, be willing to walk away. Care . . . but not thaaaaaaat much!

Information. Know all you can about a property, the area, rental history, and future value before you lock in. Use contingencies to buy yourself the time you'll need to learn all you can. You can't know everything, but get as close to everything as you can.

Price. The deal of the decade comes around once a week. Understand, the lowest price alone . . . does not a deal make. You won't have "won" the negotiation if you get a rock bottom price on a money pit. I have paid above what I was advised for a property with the right information in hand, and it's paid dividends.

Yes, you don't want to leave money on the table, you want the best price you can get. Be careful not to pay the lowest price for the biggest dump. Begin to employ these tactics today in small areas of your daily life. In my professional real estate practice and investment strategy, a successful negotiation is defined as win/win. Both parties get what they want (maybe not *everything*). Remember to always be willing to walk away from the table!

Care—but not thaaaaaat much!

My Next Step

Buy — Hold — Manage (repeat 4X)

There are no limitations to the mind except those we acknowledge. Both poverty and riches are the offspring of thought

—Napoleon Hill

In my book, *The Backyard Millionaire*, the protagonist, August, is confronted with a choice. Remain in his current station of life or change his thoughts and literally change his life. "As a man thinketh, so is he in his heart."

The Millionaire Maker is a guide to becoming a *millionaire*. Yes, it's a blueprint, and if you follow it, you'll have at least one million dollars in real estate assets. The key word isn't *millionaire*! The most important part of this guide is a subtle yet powerful word: *becoming*. Jim Rohn famously said, "If I hand you a million dollars, you'd better hurry up and become a millionaire."

Wait! If you hand me a million bucks, I would already be a millionaire, right? Wrong. Money alone does not a millionaire make. It is in the becoming that you learn to keep, grow, and sustain wealth. Look at the generational fortunes that are so often squandered by the recipients who never learned to become. Hence the expression, shirt sleeves to shirt sleeves in three generations. Granddad builds a fortune and hands it down to his kid, who squanders it before the grandkid can get his hands on it

The steps in this guide are built to help you learn to think and act like a millionaire no matter what your current bank balance says. When you apply these tactics to your daily life, you will achieve any level of success you set for yourself. Be it a million dollars, or twenty million. If you adhere to these six steps, you will win. You will become a millionaire.

Buy and Hold = Gold

Change your thoughts, change your life.
— Norman Vincent Peale

Allow me to share a painful story with you. Again, take notes so you don't make the same mistakes we did. Tiffanie and I built a commercial building for our young pottery business. We sold our retail company so we could focus on wholesale production. In so doing, we converted our commercial space into a terrific home. We'd been managing the apartment building where we lived for seven years, and we were ready for a home of our own.

Tiffanie redesigned the open industrial space into a wonderful three-bedroom two-bath home. We loved it. Close enough to the ocean we could hear the waves and walk to the beach in a few minutes. We outgrew the house, and frankly, the area was a little too commercial to raise our girls in. We decided it was time to move. A wonderful older ranch-style home on the ocean became available, and we could afford it.

After we had put the deal together for the oceanfront home, a bit of panic set in. We needed to sell the other house as quickly as possible. Our thinking was, "We can't afford to own two homes. What if we ever have a vacancy? We would have *two* mortgage payments to make." With thinking like that, we were right. Who we were at that time couldn't afford to own two homes. With our limiting beliefs, we were in fact precluded from owning more than one home. Even though we already did.

We had purchased the home on the ocean, and Tiffanie needed months to renovate it before we could actually move in. Meanwhile, we continued living in our original home while making *two* mortgage payments. Our brains were so wired for having only *one* payment and *one* home, we couldn't see what was in front of us.

To make a long story short, we made a large profit in selling the commercial house. Nearly eighty thousand dollars. That was an absolute fortune to us. We had been doing fine with our business, but there was never more than a month's reserves on hand. So, to have a sudden influx of this kind of cash was life-changing.

Here's the rest of the story: The day I handed the keys over to the buyer, I learned a million-dollar lesson. I asked him what they were going to do with it. He said with almost no humility (good for him), "Oh, it's already rented. The tenant moves in tomorrow."

"Who's your tenant?" I asked, shocked he'd already found someone.

"The State of Alaska."

"What?"

"Yes, the State is leasing the building for offices."

My heart skipped a beat. Dare I ask for how much? Yes, I dared and then my heart sank. You see, the new tenant, a state agency, was to be paying a rent in exactly double the amount of what our mortgage payment was.

Had we been of a mind to hold the home, we too could have been the landlord to that State agency. As I tell you this story, twenty-plus years later, that same tenant is still there. No doubt the rent has stepped up numerous times. Not to mention that we had only fifteen years left to pay on our mortgage.

In doing the math, we lost hundreds of thousands of dollars in rental income. Not to mention another three hundred thousand dollars (at least) in appreciation. While we sold the building at top dollar for the day, we had no idea what was to become of the area. It became a desirable and valuable market within our overall market.

What keeps me from slamming my head into the keyboard as I type? Glad you asked! Yes, we lost a fortune by not having the vision to see what was possible. What we learned in that compressed period of time has earned us a fortune worth millions of dollars since. If it had taken the new buyer months or longer to find a suitable tenant, we wouldn't have had a shocking ice-bath realization. If it had taken years for his investment to begin to pay dividends, we might have missed the major lesson that would alter the rest of our lives.

We began to think differently in that exact moment. We now buy and hold. If we sell a property, it's with full knowledge of where the proceeds are going. The only reason we sell is to reinvest in a property that we know will earn us more income, appreciation, and long-term value.

Never again have we felt ourselves not capable of more. We are backyard millionaires who own commercial buildings, apartment buildings, and single-family homes. Change your thoughts, change your life. You are only as limited as you think. There is no one holding you back from your dreams except you. It's easy to look back and trace the tracks of our years. What about going forward? What if you have tried to think anew? What if you've read the books, taken the courses, but failed to take action? Go back to step two. Look closely at your circle. Who is in your circle that is breathing life into you? Who is there to help you hold yourself accountable? As you make your plans for becoming a backyard millionaire, read and reread these foregoing steps. Apply the plan, take action today. Start right now to become a millionaire. Remember, own and control at least four homes in your area and you will be a millionaire. Imagine having just four homes that you own outright by the time you retire, earning cash flow for you. How might your future look different? Perhaps you already own HOME 1, then it's time to acquire HOME 2. Talk with your mortgage broker about your options for HOME 2—buy another home as your primary and move into it (lower down payment), or acquire HOME 2 with an investor loan.

The right mortgage broker is going to make *all* the difference as you apply this plan to your life.

My Next Step

_____

_____

_____

_____

_____

_____

_____

_____

_____

_____

_____

_____

Enter the Mastermind

Napoleon Hill, a towering figure in the landscape of personal development and success philosophy, invested substantial thought and insight into unraveling the transformative power embedded within the concept of masterminds. This exploration into the synergy of collective intelligence stands as a foundational pillar in understanding how individuals can propel each other to unprecedented heights. Hill, with his keen understanding of the human psyche, articulated the phenomenon where two or more individuals, consciously gathering with the shared objective of elevating one another, generate a collaborative force that transcends the sum of its individual parts. In this fusion of minds, a third entity emerges—an entity that surpasses the confines of individual thinking, and in doing so, unlocks the gateway to what Hill aptly described as infinite intelligence.

The intricacies of this profound concept are a rich tapestry woven with insights and wisdom. Hill postulated that the combined mental faculties of a group, united by a common purpose, create a reservoir of ideas and creativity that far exceeds what any single mind can generate. The mastermind principle, as articulated by Hill, accentuates the idea that the collective energy, knowledge, and creativity generated within such a group become accessible to each member.

Now, consider the invitation extended to you, an invitation to be an integral part of our Backyard Millionaire Mastermind. This is more than an invitation—it's an opportunity to immerse yourself in a community of like-minded individuals. Envision a cohort of ambitious and forward-thinking people, diligently working towards the realization of their future fortunes. Picture the power of shared goals, diverse perspectives, and collaborative efforts converging to shape a collective destiny. The Backyard Millionaire Mastermind is not merely a group—it's a dynamic force committed to propelling each member towards financial success and personal fulfillment.

As you embark on this transformative journey, guided by the six steps meticulously laid out in this comprehensive guide, you'll find yourself not merely on a path but on an expressway towards your financial goals. These steps are more than a roadmap—they constitute a blueprint for success, carefully crafted to streamline your progress and eliminate years of trial and error. By diligently following these steps, you're not merely inching forward—you're making leaps, propelling yourself towards your desired destination.

Yet, for those whose ambition knows no bounds and who seek to expedite their trajectory even further, an avenue exists to attain

greater momentum—the Backyard Millionaire Mastermind. Becoming a part of this ex-
clusive circle is not just a strategic move—it's a
commitment to supercharge your progress. It's
an acknowledgment that achieving extraordi-
nary success is not a solitary pursuit but a collaborative endeavor.

The fundamental belief underpinning the
Backyard Millionaire Mastermind is that the
journey to financial prosperity is not one that
should be undertaken alone. The power of collective intelligence, diverse experiences, and
shared insights can propel individuals towards
success with unparalleled speed and precision.
The Backyard Millionaire Mastermind pro-
vides a platform for members to share their
challenges, celebrate their victories, and learn
from the collective wisdom of the group.

Now, let's reflect on the notion that you
were born on purpose and with a purpose. This
profound realization, rooted in the teachings
of personal development, underscores the idea

that each individual has a unique calling—a distinct contribution to make to the world. The definite chief aim in life, as espoused by Napoleon Hill and echoed by countless success philosophers, is not merely a lofty goal but a clarion call to align one's actions, thoughts, and aspirations with a higher purpose.

In essence, the Backyard Millionaire Mastermind serves as a conduit for individuals to actualize their purpose. It's not just about financial success; it's about holistic success—success that encompasses health, wealth, and prosperity in the truest sense. This mastermind is a space where individuals are not just encouraged to dream big but are provided with the tools, strategies, and collective support to turn those dreams into reality.

Consider, for a moment, your current position on the ladder of life. Regardless of your standing, the fundamental truth remains—you can ascend higher. The journey towards financial success, towards becoming a backyard millionaire, is not reserved for a select few. It's an invitation extended to all those who dare to dream, to aspire, and to take action.

As you contemplate this invitation, envision the many millions awaiting you. These millions are not merely financial; they encompass opportunities, experiences, and a life of abundance. The Backyard Millionaire Mastermind isn't just about accumulating wealth— it's about creating a life that aligns with your purpose and aspirations.

In closing, I extend my heartfelt wishes for your health, wealth, and prosperity. May this transformative journey, guided by the principles of the backyard millionaire philosophy, bring you not only financial success but also a profound sense of fulfillment and purpose. Remember, you are not alone on this journey. The collective power of the Backyard Millionaire Mastermind is here to propel you towards the life you envision.

Acknowledgments

Thank you to the amazing team that helped bring this book to you:

✦ Tiffanie Story—My Muse and First Reader.

✦ Marthy Johnson—The most patient editor I could ask for.

✦ Lori Weidert—An Independent Author's best friend from A–Z.

✦ Liz Shallenberger—Wickedly great cover art and design.

About the Author

CHRIS STORY resides in Homer, Alaska. He is an author, speaker, real estate investor, and owner/Broker of Story Real Estate, as well as host of the Backyard Millionaire Radio Show (podcast available on iTunes and Spotify).

Chris is a lifelong Alaskan, married to his high school sweetheart, Tiffanie. Together they have raised their two daughters, Ashley and Zoe in Homer, Alaska.

Connect with Chris

Chris Story
1005 Carriage Court
Homer Alaska 99603
(907)299.7653
Email: AlaskaMattersRadio@gmail.com